Poems of Here to There and Everywhere

Art Schmitz

Ten|16
PRESS

www.ten16press.com - Waukesha, WI

For information, please contact:

Ten|16
PRESS

www.ten16press.com
Waukesha, WI

To Nancy, my patient wife, who had to put up with the times I spent composing these poems and then listening to the original and final versions.

A Bird

One flew over the Cuckoo's Nest
And this is what it saw
I don't know about the rest
But it wasn't a cat's paw

Its name is cuculus caronis
How's that for a fancy moniker
Because of the sounds its calls is
The Cuckoo call is a monitor

A Great Life

It's a great life
If you don't weaken
But Mama, who wants to be strong
It's so nice if you do it right
But what of us who do wrong?

A Lunar Fantasy

The moon and I were full last night
The moon with green cheese
And I with Miller Lite

The glow of the moon
On our very young faces
Cast its spell
On our lovers embraces

It wasn't Blueberry Hill
As we hugged and kissed
We still got our thrill
With nothing amiss

A Periodical Question

The erudite environment was enveloped
With the pursuit of periodical investigation
The constant sober mien of the human dignity
Performing her vital duties of serious consequence
Recording, lending, questioning, directing
And returning transactions of periodical literature
For a single cataclysmic moment of beauty rare
Revealed an inner transcendental joy
In serving all
As with august respect for mankind's urgent quest for knowledge
She directed the little boy to the restroom
At the end of the adjacent hall

A Quiet Interest

Why haven't I done this before
A poem about something I like to do
It's not like a thing with a roar
But a pleasure always anew

They're tiny pieces of paper
But boy the subjects they cover
From an Austrian boy's naked caper
To what scientists have discovered

They come in varied hues
Some dull and some very bright
Of subjects no longer news
With scenes of both day and night

And in case you're still in ignorance
Of what this is all about
It's all about collecting stamps
And doing it with rarely a shout

A Taste of Spring

The grass is green
The sky is blue
The rising sun
A brilliant hue

The air is warm
The leaves are green
I can hear the birds
Although unseen

The breeze blows soft
Against my face
Spring has sprung
For the human race

A Transition

He was an ornery 8-year-old brat
Who thought he knew where it was at
He sometimes hit his lovin' cousin
Because he thought that she was buggin' him

He soon learned how to really swear
And it wasn't just a kid's hot air
He could also do an angry pout
When he was more than just put out

He also had some very good points
Even when he was out of joint
He loved his little feline pets
Treating them to the very best

Spanking always put his body in knots
Over Pa's very hard-muscled knee
And that's how that terrible ornery tot
Eventually turned out to be me

A Winter Day

The mercury's at 25 above, Fahrenheit
    There's six inches of snow on the ground
Clouds hang below the gray sky above
    Barely letting the light of dawn show through

It's only a half hour drive to Pewaukee Lake
    Another fifteen minutes to drive out on the ice
Listening to the crunch of snow under the wheels
    Before stopping to unload the gear

A few more minutes to drill three holes
    Through a couple of feet of solid ice
Watching my breath a wisp of steam
    A sense of open freshness in the air

Eyeballing the bobbers sitting quiet in each hole
    The silvery streak of a passenger train
A momentary distraction on the north shore
    Before a bobber slowly sinks from view

A certain sign of a fish on the end of the line
    Hooked on a waxie for bait
A slab-sided crappie pulled up and out
    Flipping itself in a dying frenzy on the ice

Followed by more, bluegills and perch
    Bloodying the snow away from the holes
The day dies in a mauve haze in the west
    Refreshed inside and out I drive home

Abloom

She woke and lifted up her head
And cocked one eye which plainly said
Is someone here to look at me
Or must I cry in misery

Her glance went round and saw me there
She took the time for a longer stare
Then opened her lips in pleasure wide
And smiled as I stood by her side

Her warm and fuzzy form I took
To the shoulder and my elbow's crook
Then jauntily we turned around
To mother with a happy bound

Mother laid her down with care
And peeled off this and that from there
Revealing a red spotted shape
Of measles in its brightest state

An Aging Soliloquy

When I was just a 16-year-old kid
My life was a mixed-up world
Looking for pleasure was in all I did
In an exciting kind of social whirl

Walking for ice cream one summer evening
With a friend's mother who was cool
Going out of the house we were leaving
More pleasure was going to rule

I thought and spoke of life now and then
Hoping to always be this happy
Looking ahead to a life with no end
And spoke of my hopes snappy

A life short but happy I wanted
Was my wish for the future unknown
A life short wasn't to be granted
But happiness was greatly owned

And so beyond being quite old
I can sit back and relish the past
And know that I can be bold
And still have pleasures that last

As Exciting as Watching Grass Grow

1

A round green ball on the table sat
Ignored of course
By our old tom cat

2

Day after day on the table it laid
I eyed it with each meal I ate
But I couldn't help the attention I paid

3

One dull day I noticed a change
From the original green of the thing
To a sort of orangish range

4

The weeks slowly passed through
The thing wasn't moved a bit
The orange became a darker hue

5

And finally turned to a brilliant red
As it matured to its final form
A ripe tomato fully bred

Being Useless

I love being useless
It suits me just great
Others serve as pressed
While I just sit and wait

They set stuff on the table
All kinds of tasty good food
It's not just an ancient fable
Putting me in a restful mood

There's the fine china ware
And the silver's always the best
The others are very aware
That my ways are always at rest

It's Christmas time for everyone
Of which I'm the oldest you know
They don't mind me resting my bum
Saving my energy to go

Bessie's Birthday Poem

Bessie's a gardener par excellence
She's also a wonderful cook
She doesn't need dirt at a fence
Or have to look at a book

Today is her special day
For all of us to enjoy
So we wish you a happy birthday
As we celebrate with joy

Blood and Peace

The history of man is a bloody one
The first man's son was the first one done
To death by his father's firstborn son

So what we're seeing in our town
Is really nothing new around
The constant hope for a future sound

Without the impulse violent
Of guns and knives
In malice bent

There are many a folk
Who live their lives
Without a poke

They know no violence
And live in peace
But not in silence

They know how to talk
Without any anger
And at violence balk

Blue Stars Turn to Gold

In homes across the USA
A star in blue is shown
All too often comes the blow
And the Blue Star turns to Gold

The tank is on an Iraq road
An IED explodes
The troops inside are gone
And Blue Stars turn to Gold

Airborne men in their chopper
Survey the scene below
A rocket splits the aircraft
And Blue Stars turn to Gold

A shot is heard
The Afghan sunset glows
Friendly fire the paper says
And a Blue Star turns to Gold

When the folks in uniform come
The day may be hot or cold
They're there to have their duty done
And the Blue Star turns to Gold

Mother, Father, Sister, Brother
Wife and children
Sometimes young or very old
Another Blue Star turns to Gold

The media shows the procession
The grief cannot be told
Taps is softly sounded
The Blue Star's turned to Gold

The days go by
The months unfold
No matter the years
The Blue Star's turned to Gold

Borrowed Time

I went into George Webb's
Not too many years ago
It was where my appetite led
For me it was usual you know

Soon an older man came in
He looked somewhat decrepit
His face had a permanent grin
Which did the old man credit

Seated on the closest stool
He stared my way for a time
Saying, "I don't you're a fool
Your eyes have a healthy shine"

He told me he was eighty-one
And could I equal that
I said I could, and still have fun
At eighty-two and a half

Don't you feel, he said to me
That you're living on borrowed time
Not as long as I can my bobber see
And a fish on the end of the line

And then I thought of life and death
Of birth and the joy of living
The scope of life's great breadth
Of getting and of giving

Finally coming to the decision
That life is a question replete
Of life being not of precision
But life being always complete

Brotherly Love

It seems like it was yesterday
But it's been years that he's been gone
As kids we had lots of interplay
It's still hard to know that's done

There's been a vacuum in my life
Where he often used to be
Sure we sometimes had strife
But we'd make it up for free

And yet, he'll always be there
In my heart and in my mind
His actions weren't always fair
But never was he unkind

By Any Other Name

We all use it every day
Now it's usually free
Years ago we often paid
Now no cost in glee

What we're doing there
If we take too long
Creates tension in the air
No one's singing a song

It's been around for many years
We've experienced it often
Sometimes its brought some tears
And sometimes feelings softened

Called a necessary many years ago
It's had a plethora of names
Most of them you already know
Whether for guys or for dames

The loo of the UK is where it's at
There are still some houses in the out
And John isn't the name of a cat
We can use the privy without a pout

A restroom it's sometimes called
For restful reading there
Or just some excuse if one's appalled
At the facts of life unfair

Another term's a bathroom
If there's a tub or shower there
Some have known a slippery gloom
As they've fallen through the air

For those of racing's sport
It's a pit stop when nature's heeded
No need of an order by a court
Especially if tissues are needed

Take a volcano and a Tory
The result when put together
A non-eruptive lavatory
In any kind of weather

Coincidence?

Today the leaves are blowing wild
The city's trees are nearly bare
The autumn weather's almost mild
The rakes are ready to do their share

But I wonder as the weather changes
If it's by chance the tree's leaves fall
Or is this a sign of God's great ranges
That the wind strips trees that are short or tall

Soon the trees will all be stripped
Of their leaves now on the ground
In the country they'll be riveted
To enhance the soil around

When the warmth of spring time comes
Once again the trees will green
And the country's moisture runs
The soil beneath will be richer seen

Is this God's way of being sure
That all things living can survive
As nature's cycles run as pure
Leaves being the sign that trees are alive

Computer Technology and Me

Cable not connected
On my monitor it said
My computer's been affected
It might as well be dead

I cannot open any file
With words or with statistics
My being now is riled
With such computer logistics

This isn't the first problem I've had
There was the computer that crashed
The loss of vital data was more than bad
Myriad hopes and dreams were dashed

Contention

I'm a contentious son-of-a-gun
I love to argue
It's so much fun
I don't care if I win or lose
As long as we can share our views

Your ideas may differ from mine
As long as we show respect for each other
Making sure we don't cross a line
That would demean one or the other

Every Day is Saturday

Stayed up till midnight last night
Didn't get up till ten
The sun was shining bright
My eyes were almost open then

Didn't worry about going to church
That couldn't happen today
Not in the middle of a week search
Sunday was the day to pray

No alarm clock to ring
It's time to get up for work
Only to hear the birdies sing
The joy of nature's work

Now to roll over again
And grab a few more z's
Before I actually rise and then
To stretch my bod at ease

Is retirement great or what
For lazy folks like me
When every day is Saturday
And all my time is free

The Ford Tri-Motor

When I was a ten-year-old kid
We walked to Curtis-Wright airport
It wasn't the first time we did
It was kind of a Saturday sport

But this time into the hangars we got
We had the run of the place
We got to sit in the seats of the pilots
And flew in a fantasy race

Our favorite plane of the time
Was a Ford Tri-motor at rest
It lent itself to a rhyme
To the day that was one of the best

Years later in Kalamazoo
I again sat in a Ford Tri-motor
But this time it actually flew
As I watched 3 props do the rotor

Gene's Birthday

Bon Anniversaire

Another year's gone by it seems
A few hopes dashed
But some fulfilled dreams

In any case you can appreciate
Life's little blessings
Like the great food you ate

And now a time to look ahead
At the pleasures that's yours
When you arise from your bed

So have some fun on your day
And all the days after
We're happy to say

HAPPY BIRTHDAY GENE
From Boyce and Nancy

Green Light

Two cars at speeds too high
　　　Met at the intersection
For one car the green was the light
　　　The other had a red rejection

The car with the red went through
　　　The car with the green took the hit
From the car with the red as it flew
　　　And a life was lost in a minute

It's happened again and again
　　　Because the law is just a term
To many drivers, women and men
　　　Who couldn't care less if others get burned

Happy Birthday Harold

Harold's a versatile man of skill
Of carving wood
Of Bible knowledge and God's will
And doing good

To his neighbors he's always kind
And gentle with his friends
He knows what's on his mind
But doesn't like loose ends

He keeps his friends for years
And values their good sense
He knows of life and tears
And how to make amends

To Harold, Happy Birthday
From some old, old friends
May this be a very happy day
With many more to spend

Ice Fishing

The mercury 20 above
I'm ready for the sport I love
The fish are waiting there for me
Below the solid ice I see

I ready my electric drill
To open my 3 holes that fill
With water and floating ice chips
Cut from the ice holes' outer lips

For each hole a different bait
I drop it in each hole and wait
A tiny float sinks slowly, when
Rod and I have a fish again

I'm From

I'm from an alte Deutsche seit
And a stubborn Polish scene
That sounded like a ready fight
But turned out to be serene

I'm from a great music love
As well as a drama keen
That lift my spirits high above
And give me thoughts to dream

I'm from a love of sky and sea
With boats to sail away
To often fish my life to be
And revel in the joy each day

Killing Time

I've a persistent endeavor
To pursue a useless thing forever
To count the cars always passing by
And forgetting the numbers as I try

To find out which there are more of
Black, White, Grey or sort of
Which no one else could care about
Of my efforts while I pout

But this I can truthfully say before going
I really don't care how
Other folks feel about what I'm doing
For constant effort I'll take a bow

Lake Michigan

I drove along the lake today
One of my favorite drives
The water hits the shore in spray
As the crashing waves arrive

The sky above is blue
The water's a bluish green
As distance changes its hue
Like colors in a dream

The east winds are blowing wild
Causing white caps flowing free
In a turbulence not mild
On rocky shores and stolid trees

But further out one can see
Beyond the earth-toned surface
A brilliant water free
Of any windy disturbance

The horizon's a clear blue line
Where the sky and the water meet
And earth and sky define
The horizon a factor neat

Midsummer Carol

Tis the season for construction
Leading to my car's destruction
Fa la la, la la la la

First the tires
Then the wheels
Fa la la, la la la la

Then the chassis
That I feel
Fa la la, la la la la

Then the body
Begins to go
Fa la la, la la la la

It's gonna cost me
This I know
Fa la la, la la la la

My Gardening Experience

Mother loved her garden
If I would do the digging
I'd begun to dig without being ardent
The shovel's work had my dripping

Then I saw some earthworms
The bait I could use for fishing
In anticipation I began to squirm
Leaving the shovel in the garden sitting

No Guess Work

If you want to come along
I will know
Because it's not wrong
I will know

If you don't like the place
I will know
Because it's a different face
I will know

And if the food isn't that good
I will know
Because of your change in mood
I will know

When you want to go home again
I will know
Because your look says when
I will know

On It, In It, and Out of It

The end of a warm August day
The water of Green Bay inviting
My canoe to cruise the bay
A bit of a breeze was biting

The sun glistening on the deep blue surface
Was a beckoning call to be out on it
The white crest of a breaking waves purpose
Led us to launch our canoe going with it

My young Boy Scout friend
Paddled the stern position
I was up at the bow's end
We were in good condition

The wind some waves were making
As we paddled out on the bay
We thrilled at the way we were taking
The rises and falling away

The water was bluish green
Except for the waves as they'd crest
They had a silvery sheen
Till they'd rise up and then rest

I paddled the right side
My friend paddled the other
When we readied to ride
Back to shore to have supper

On the right side I stayed
But my friend did so too
And now we displayed
A now off-balanced crew

As we swung to the left
We quartered a wave
And of stability bereft
It was too late to save

A quick flip of a paddle
And down deep we drew
Into the drink skedaddled
We sunk below view

As I slid down into the deep
I could see the beauty of the waters blue
A lighter shade where the sun could see
And a deeper tone of a greenish hue

It felt pretty good against my skin
While I struggled to rise to the top
My water-soaked clothes were akin
For my body an anchor to drop

My right hand held my paddle
A life jacket was in my left
My young friend in panic was addled
Of his life jacket he was bereft

My young friend grasped as he could
Our canoe full of water
As the wind blew us out from the woods
And we wondered about what we oughter

Do to ease our predicament some
To the thwarts we tied our clothes
My young friend to each side clung
While I got in with my paddle to close

The distance between us and our campsite
Waving to other boats we could see
Until finally one came to toss a line tight
To tow us to water less deep

Nearing the rocky shoreline
Our feet on the bottom appeared
Walking now to the canoe
We found our clothes had disappeared

Now unclothed completely
We had little choice
But to walk the canoe in bleakly
As other campers gave us their voice

Osakis

Osakis is an Indian name
There are two places it shares
One is a town without much fame
The other's a lake that's rare

The town's not big as cities go
It sits on the shore of the lake
That lures a lot of people who know
It gives anglers a wonderful take

Pilgrims

The road is filled with them
The old, the young, and in between
Young kids, women, and a lot of men
And more than a few cocky teens

Some move faster than others
Most know where they're going
Whether they're fathers or mothers
They seem to know what they're doing

Some are dressed to fashion's hilt
Others couldn't care less
Many are physically well built
Their suits very well pressed

The younger ones seem to move fast
Most of the older move slower
But even they sometimes pass
As those before them glower

The pilgrim more driven
Will sometimes pass on the right
Scaring the righteous given
An opinion of a human blight

And, if you haven't guessed it
We're talking about cars on the road
And their drivers giving a fit
To many others driving a load

Some of their vehicles are very new
Others have seen better days
But many of them are driven askew
Among drivers who tend to laws obey

Poems

Poems are words that often rhyme
Many people enjoy them
They've been written over time
By literate men and women

For poets it's a labor of love
To find the word that'll rhyme
With the line just above
In place as well as in time

Often a poem is a message of sorts
Related to the poet's concerns
The words are the tools of great import
Written on the poet's terms

Any idea can be poetified
From the most esoteric concepts
To the mundane idea satisfied
In the writer's poetic mindset

Some poems are short
And many are too long
Few if any amount to a tort
For the poet can do no wrong

Quoth Whatever Evermore

With a handy key and a length of wire
A word for STOP is forever more
With a brief set of words to inspire
Quoth the telegraph evermore

Later coming to human kind
The phone at home and in the store
To challenge words in people's minds
Quoth the phone forevermore

Then the big screen at the show
In black and white the drama's lore
The hero always dealt the blow
Quoth the movie evermore

Then the next thing came along
We couldn't see, but heard the roar
Of many voices loud and strong
Quoth the radio forevermore

Not much more time was passed
A smaller screen came in the door
We saw and heard the news at last
Quoth the TV evermore

Then a small phone got our ear
We could carry from door to door
It became a gadget dear
Quoth the cell phone evermore

Sibling Rivalry

If a family has more than one kid
It makes for some interesting times
Disagreements pop open a lid
When some kid crosses the lines

If a kid's the oldest of two
The next kid's younger than that one
Sometimes there's a middle one too
The mix can be more than some fun

Often there's two against one
But that can change by the minute
When something wrong gets done
Who gets the blame for doing it?

It sounds like a terrible thing
But there's a learning of how to deal
The lessons have a potent ring
For living as a grownup will feel

Snow

Snow-covered trees
Tower over the walk
While kids trample their feet
As they yell and talk

It's winter fun great
With snowballs to throw
At another kid's fate
As a target to know

Swipe Your Card

I hope you don't mind
Me wasting your time
While I try to find
The words that'll rhyme

I've seen some signs
That make me wonder
About the current times
And a semantic blunder

The signs read as follows
For everyone to see
Swipe your card as it allows
Your getting cash not free

I always thought of swipe
As a criminal act of theft
But now it's words are trite
And of meaning quite bereft

And swipe can mean a whisk
Of a cloth to do a clean
Move across a disk
Or on a big machine

Then of course, there's slide
That actually isn't trite
It's not a matter of pride
But an accurate sense of right

The Caffeinated Revolution

Nuke the coffee
Will you hon?
Of course my dear
It's always fun

I place the cup
In the middle of the plate
Press the time it's up
It won't be late

The timer sounds
No light, it's dark
The handle's around
At the back it's parked

No matter where the cup I place
The handle's going to be
Somewhere in the backfield space
Because the user is me

The Calm

The place seems the same
Inside and out
But a subtle change
Has come about

Softer are sounds
From out of doors
Cozier everything
Ceilings to floors

Quiet the flowers
On the table spread soft
Warm is the air
The storm is aloft

The Diletante

I'm not a jack of all trades
I'm also master of none
I often try to make the grade
And still have a lot of fun

I've recorded some events of life
Maybe writing a poem or two
I've encountered peace as well as strife
While always thinking anew

I'm sometimes active with muscle
But enjoy the quiet life as well
I can, if there's a vital need hustle
And let my mind on thoughts dwell

But the truth of the matter
When it comes down to that
I can enjoy idle chatter
With words, skinny or fat

The GI Bill

Walking into the house one day
I heard my mother to my brother say
Why don't you go for the GI Bill
Like your older brother Boyce will

Ma, he said, in a voice with pride
I don't need the GI Bill to ride
He doesn't know how to do anything
He just saves stamps and sings

In the navy I became a diesel mechanic
All he did was type stuff with clicks
I've now a skill I can use in the shop
What'll he do if the GI Bill stops

In the navy I was a diesel man
All he did was get a tan
Now I've a trade to work for pay
He needs the GI Bill to make his way

The GREAT Move

Forty-five years in our home
A place of comfort when we were down
It was always there after we roamed
The best place for us in our town

And now we're in a different place
It's called an apartment now
It's nice, but doesn't have the space
For all the junk that time's endowed

Believe it or not I really like it here
It's cozy but in a different way
I don't have to do stairs to get a beer
Or to the attic for my computer play

No matter the weather for our car
Is in the heated garage downstairs
We can still see the sky with stars
And nobody has to put on airs

The Growth Continuum

Growing up is sometimes slow
And sometimes fast
But always in doing so
Creates a past

We learn to walk
And often cry
We begin to talk
And new things try

We soon realize
We're not all the same
It's not just our eyes
Our genders have names

Boys are different than girls
Their bodies have different parts
It's not just the girls with curls
Curiosity becomes an art

It's something of a shock
When we learn how we're created
It makes our being rock
And then we duplicate it

The Most Dangerous Thing in the World

We see it everywhere
There's nothing with it to compare
Perfectly innocuous it seems
But often it affects our dreams

No country is an exception
To the problems of its conception
But we can't get along without it
Because of how we flout it

Now where did I put the thing
I know it caught on my ring
I know it's there somewhere
I wish I had a pair

Then I wouldn't have to look
And waste the time it took
To rummage through
All the papers askew

So what is this object
So problematic
It's any surface
That's flat, not erratic

The Passenger Train

Whenever I see a passenger train
I want to be riding on it
As its wheels ride the rails
With the rhythm of a sonnet

I don't care its destination
Just the feel of the motion
Gives me a sensation
Of moving locomotion

Sitting in a comfortable seat
Watching the scenery roll by
Is a feeling that can't be beat
No matter the look of the sky

And when it stops at a station
The sense of motion is gone
I feel a sense of elation
That I can go on until done

And when it's time to eat
Walking to the dining car
Getting there's a treat
Riding along thus far

Eating a well-cooked meal
The view outside is roving
While we savor the flavor real
Our train is really moving

When I reach the final place
I gather my things for leaving
But my wish is still to grace
My train seat with my being

The Perfect Winter Day

The sky looks gray through a frosted window
    An inner smile softens the hard lines of a wrinkled face
Slipping hairy legs into insulated underwear
    A snowmobile suit over everything else

Checking the fishing gear in the pickup
    The mercury in the mid-twenties
A gentle west wind blowing
    Fishing the crisp snow-covered ice would be easy

Driving west to the lake with anticipation
    Going easy on the gas pedal
Morning rush hour traffic no problem
    A brief stop at Smokey's for bait

A dozen crappie minnows for starters
    A box of waxies to go with it
A few suckers for the big fish
    Spikes, wigglers, and mousies as well

Stopping at the now abandoned launch ramp
    Too busy with boats on Pewaukee Lake
In the heat of summer's revved up action
    It's quiet now with winter's slower pace

Scanning the horizon to check out the view
  Groups of men, tents, vehicles, and shanties
In the distance, contemplating the big question
  Walk or chance driving out on the ice

Easing the truck off the ramp to the lake's edge
  Unfastening the seat belt and opening a window
Just in case there's a weak spot out there
  Opening the door for escape will be easier

Shifting into four-wheel drive for better traction
  Steering onto the tracks of preceding vehicles
Keeping the speed to ten miles an hour
  Hearing the crushing sound of wheels on crisp snow

Over the bumpy rutted snowy surface
  Watching for tell-tale signs of soft ice
Dipping into a deeper trough of the path
  Bouncing back onto the regular track

Passing the starkly barren tree studded island
  To follow the way of the others
Toward Taylor Bay near Pewaukee's north shore
  Slowing down for a closer look

To find, if possible, some open holes
      But, it's too early in the day
Nobody's gone home with their catch
      No big deal, the auger's in the back

Parking, so the wind's from behind
      Pulling the plastic sled from the truck
Placing the new power auger just bought
      With the bucket of rods and bait from the shop

Rejecting the claustrophobic confines
      Of a shanty or a tent's four walls and a roof
For the freedom of space and sight
      Of the fresh air and open sky above

Two hands holding the auger upright
      Sure to keep it on the vertical straight
A touch on the black button of the power head
      The vibrant spin of the spiraling blades

The sudden surge as the blade goes through
      Turning off the power to pull it back up
Leaving an even six-inch hole open
      Full of a mix of snow, ice, and water

One hole drilled through two feet of ice
        Skimmed clear of snow and slush
Clear water rising to the surface
        Blade-marked rings show in the hole

A bobber slowly sinks from the surface
        A crappie for sure, the rod tip bends down
The feel of the fish fighting the pull of the rod
        The flash of silver, a splash of water

The first fish of the day removed from the hook
        A glistening slab in a flipping frenzy on the ice
Its last meal was the minnow it swallowed too fast
        Now the re-bait the line for the next try

Time to drill the third hole for more
        Chances to vary the bait presented
To a piscine smorgasbord
        Tempting to the palates below the surface

Another bobber slowly sinking away
        This time needs a careful retrieve
There's a sucker on the hook, could be a biggie
        The rod bends way down, maybe a northern

A strong pull on the line
    Moving in circles below
A long snake-like shape comes into view
    A pull, a splash, and it's out of sight

The rod hits the snow on the ice
    The hook, sinker, and bait are gone
As is the malevolent eye of the northern pike
    Re-baiting will wait for a lull

More bites, more fish, some nice bluegills on waxies
    Even a few jumbo perch join the catch
A pause now and then between bites
    A keeper bass on a shiner

A small mouth large enough
    To swallow the minnow whole
The iridescent mother-of-pearl beauty
    Within the lips of the fish under its tongue

The wind's changed to the east
    The gray cloudy sky has cleared
No more bites, the bobbers float still
    The sun a bright red orange glow in the west

The temperature's dropped, the gloves go on
        Before fingers freeze in the windy chill
While winding up line on the rods
        Securing hooks out of the way

It's getting dark, a soft mauve tinge in the sky
        Picking up the fish to be cleaned
Whistling, re-loading the back of the truck
        Before the drive to the shore

Twinkling lights of the distant village
        Tracks on the ice invisible in the dark
The heater and defroster are on
        Driving a slow and cautious ride

Then following pinpoint tail lights of another car
        To the ramp and back on solid ground
Stopping at George Webb's for a burger and jo
        To celebrate the perfect winter day

The Power of Steam

I rode in comfort in my train
Pulled by a steam engine sturdy
A smooth ride with no pain
Sometimes it gets me there early

I saw another train going west
Also pulled by an engine with steam
For many years steam was the best
It fostered many a boyish dream

Watching it chugging with all its might
Inseminating the virginal blue sky above
With shapeless wisps of snowy white
It was the symbol of my traveling love

The Real Thing

It was mid-December 1944
When Sarge barged in the barracks door
The division's hot was what he said
Now get your asses out of bed

It was only a week I'd been in France
The miserable days were cold and bad
But as of now I was in a trance
With nothing to make me feel very glad

The thought of going to a combat zone
Froze my being to the very core
Now I wished that I was home
And Sarge hadn't opened the door

Into the showers now we went
We didn't know when the next one would be
No letters home could now be sent
Because of tight security

All non-essentials went into bag B
Our weapons had to be cleaned
We would need them very soon you see
A careful and deliberate process it seemed

The day went far too fast for me
A quite hasty deal of paper stuff
Requisitioning live ammo to be
Soon to be used if things got rough

Dusk eventually came to the scene
As formations boarded the trucks
A situation much less than serene
Someone was heard to say, "this sucks."

In the darkness cold we rode
Further away from home base
Along the dark narrow country roads
With miles of blackout lights ablaze

Many men found comfort in sleep
A lot of other guys smoked
Some of the guys were seen to weep
Their fearful spirits nearly broke

We rode through unknown small towns
That had been bombed and seen awful things
But they'd experienced a rebound
And we heard some of the people sing

Our 35-mile convoy kept moving fast
Like a black snake that's hungry
A target for the Luftwaffe to blast
A blow for their here hated country

Seemingly in the middle of nowhere
Our truck suddenly stopped in the dark
We jumped off the back to somewhere
It was definitely not going to be a lark

The pitch black dark sky above
Was loudly being rent asunder
With no thoughts of kindly love
From artillery blasts of thunder

Separated soon from the others
Mac and I stayed on the spot
We'd become almost like brothers
As we shared the fear of our lot

Standing still alone in the night
We decided to try to get some sleep
Crawling into our sleeping bags tight
No watch did we think to keep

The next morning we both awoke
And quickly moved away fast
Parked on either side of us no joke
Two Sherman tanks ready to blast

Late in the afternoon of that day
We finally found our outfit
We knew there'd be some hell to pay
Because we'd been far out of it

Doing outpost duty later that night
We shuddered outside of a building place
Fearing the artillery blasts bright
Bringing tears to the cold skin of our face

Outpost duty for us always meant
Standing quite still in a place
Eyeballing the area with serious intent
Of seeing in time an enemy face

Another night of serious displacement
Hank and I had a choice to make
One was a concrete block emplacement
The other an air raid trench to take

Hank was firm for the concrete block
The concrete block was above ground
The trench gave a better safety lock
I thought as I looked around

Almost midnight a shell landed near
The earth shook more than a bit
The situation was immediately clear
An ammo dump had been hit

The next morning we saw the story
The block house was totally gone
But our trench kept us from glory
And we weren't completely undone

It was now Christmas Eve in Bastogne
An old house was our outpost site
Most of the structure was of stone
The unbroken windows were tight

The cold dismal view of the land
Presented a snowy white scene
Otherwise the landscape was bland
With naught but a few trees to be seen

When eerily suddenly up in the sky
We heard the sounds of numerous planes
They were German Junkers coming nigh
With brilliant thermal flares being rained

Grabbing our loaded weapons closer
For all the good that would do
We fell down the steps to the cellar
Praying for our endangered lives anew

We heard the blast and explosion occur
And felt the force of the impact
To go back up and check we demurred
If alive in the morning we'd react

The bomb that landed on our dwelling
Was thankfully a blessing and a dud
It hit and smashed the top of the house felling
Without the loss of any human blood

The seriously real problem we discovered
Was where the bomb was actually bound
It was nose down where it covered
The debris of the split toilet it had found

The real tragedy of the circumstance
Was our anger over the bomb's situation
This had been the only working instance
Of a toilet in our war-torn location

The Red Light Dread

The sun may shine a morning red
And so may an embarrassed face
Blushing from the awful dread
Of a totally unfortunate fate

The traffic signal lights really dread
That you know why the traffic light
Always goes from green to red
In all its crimson brilliance bright

But the reddest thing of all though
Would be your own face sweet
If you always had to stop and go
In the middle of a busy street

The Train of Life

Life's a lot like a railroad train
It starts out slow and gathers speed
The ride has its share of pain
But there's also love, a basic need

There's times we get side tracked
To let a faster train go by
We've a lot of baggage packed
To carry until we die

The slow train is often the better
There's time to see the scenery
And describe it in a letter
If it's snow or fields of greenery

We don't usually travel alone
As we ride our way through life
Others ride along as we roam
With love and a bit of strife

We lose some passengers as we ride
They've come to their final station
We recall what they meant before they died
As their lives were a celebration

And as we ride to our destination
Our train slows down to let us off
Our bodies no more a great elation
But our soul's now ready to go aloft

The Tree of Life

In Genealogy speak
Each of us is a tree
With branches and leaves
And roots to tweak

Twixt roots and leaves
We've sturdy trunks
Trees often relieve
A human's blue funk

What good is a tree
It doesn't move
It stands up free
But its shade we love

We don't have leaves
Or roots in the ground
We can laugh and grieve
And make loud sounds

Until a tree falls
To its max it has grown
But then it gives all
As wood it is known

We as humans are mobile
We tend to move around
We're not always very noble
And often make weird sounds

A tree can live long
While humans burn out
But both live a song
Of what life's all about

To Dream and Not to Dream

The Bible says old men sit and dream
   But that's not what I'm about
I'm active in several different scenes
   As if I was an active scout

I've got my share of aches and pains
   That limits what I can do
And sometimes problems come like rains
   When I do things I rue

But to sit and dream takes some time
   Away from what needs to be done
Like putting words together to rhyme
   And enjoy the effort as fun

Waste No More

Popcorn or Potato Chips
Some of the junk food we adore
Can be eaten with some dips
And then we want some more

But eating them straight
When on the floor they fall
Sometimes a mess create
Then we can't eat them at all

But some of us anyway will
Because we love the taste
The flavor's in them still
And we can't tolerate waste

What is so rare?

What's so rare as a hot day in December
Or a hard frozen lake in June
Cause the sun turned black you remember
And they've found green cheese on the moon

What's the REAL problem

Last year there were 55 shootings at this time
And almost everyone's concerned
Some think there should be higher fines
Or longer prison terms

But that's not the only problem in town
Few drivers stop for stop signs
Or even think about slowing down
Even red lights are not to mind

Kids drive without a license to drive
Why not they often say
The grownups disobey and survive
So why shouldn't I enjoy the day

Winter-Summer

Winter's a dichotomy
Between those without
Who haven't got much money
While we in comfort flout

Our homes with comfort
And inner cheer
We're cozy without effort
Outside of winter drear

The snow outside is beautiful
For us who have it made
Its pristine white is plentiful
Too much for those unpaid

At night we see the houses lit
As good folk gather there
But those with nowhere else to fit
Make do in open air

I can enjoy the winter fun
Because I've got some dough
But feel for those who have to run
For help they need to grow

Is there a solution
For winter's homeless folk
Some kind of resolution
The need is not a joke

It must be very tough
To sleep when one is cold
Out in places rough
Whether young or old

So who's to blame
For folks like this
Who live in shame
With little bliss

Summer can also be too hot
To find a place to cool
The poor folk who haven't got
The comfort of a swimming pool

What can we do to help the soul
Who needs a helping hand
To ease his comfort roll
And help him understand

That there are many others
Who really want to help
Their less fortunate brothers
In better comfort dwell

Even as a kid, Art Schmitz read poems and liked poetry. His fifth grade teacher asked him to write a poem to go with a wedding present she was giving. The next poem, "Abloom," written in 1953, was inspired by his daughter when she broke out with measles as a baby. That was followed by "A Periodical Question" inspired by a scene he witnessed at the Muskegon Public Library in 1965.

It wasn't until he was invited to a poets group meeting in Milwaukee, Wisconsin several years ago that Art began to write poems on a regular basis. "Living on Borrowed Time" appeared in *50 Plus*, a paper aimed at senior citizens, in March of 2016. "A Quiet Interest" appeared in *Across the Fence Post*, the newsletter of the Wisconsin Federation of Stamp Clubs.

The wartime poetry was inspired by experiences he recounted in his book *A Tourist in Uniform*, published in 2015.

Art retired from a 35-year career as a teacher of mentally challenged children in 1985, and he and his wife Nancy will be celebrating their 48th wedding anniversary in November 2018. Art will be turning 95 years old in October of this year.

www.ingramcontent.com/pod-product-compliance
Lightning Source LLC
Chambersburg PA
CBHW060345050426

42449CB00011B/2837